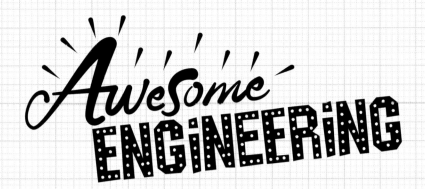

SPACECRAFT

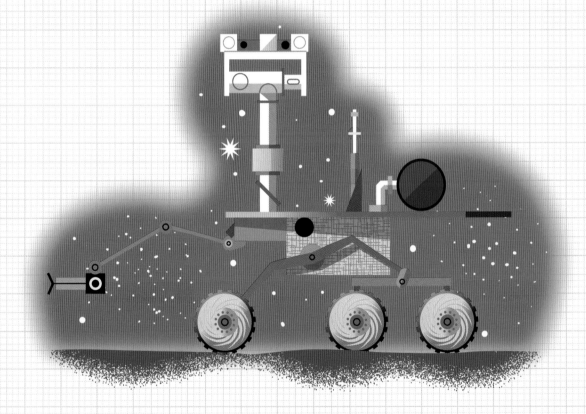

SALLY SPRAY
WITH ARTWORK BY MARK RUFFLE

W
FRANKLIN WATTS
LONDON•SYDNEY

Franklin Watts

First published in Great Britain in 2017
by The Watts Publishing Group
Copyright © The Watts Publishing Group, 2017

Series editor: Paul Rockett
Series design and illustration: Mark Ruffle
www.rufflebrothers.com
Consultant:
Andrew Woodward BEng (Hons) CEng MICE FCIArb

HB ISBN 978 1 4451 5533 3
PB ISBN 978 1 4451 5534 0

Printed in China

Franklin Watts
An imprint of
Hachette Children's Group
Part of The Watts Publishing Group
Carmelite House
50 Victoria Embankment
London EC4Y 0DZ
An Hachette UK Company
www.hachette.co.uk
www.franklinwatts.co.uk

Picture credits:
Diyana Dimitrova/Shutterstock: 29tc; ESA/
Hubble/NASA: 19bc; ESA/Rosetta/MPS for
OSIRIS Team MPS/UPD/LAM/IAA/SSO/
INTA/UPM/DASP/IDA: 20b; Elsa Hoffmann
/Shutterstock: 29tl; Yan Lev/Shuttertsock:
29tr; NASA: 13t, 17t, 23b; NASA,
ESA, and M. Livio and the Hubble 20th
Anniversary Team (STScI): 19br; NASA,
ESA, and M.H. Wong and J. Tollefson (UC
Berkeley): 19bl; NASA/JPL-Caltech/Cornell
Univ./Arizona State Univ.: 27b; Stepan
Popov/Shuttertsock: 28tl; Alexey Rotanov/
Shuttertsock: 28tr; Oleg Sam/Shuttertsock:
28tc.

MIX
Paper from
responsible sources
FSC® C104740

FSC
www.fsc.org

CONTENTS

3, 2, 1, BLAST OFF!

People have been dreaming of space travel for hundreds of years. Only in the last 80 years has our technology and engineering been advanced enough to build spacecraft that can blast off into the night sky – exploring our galaxy and beyond!

WHAT IS A SPACECRAFT?

Spacecraft can be anything made by humans sent into space to carry out a task. They can be simple communication satellites that send information to us from around the world. They can also be manned vehicles and stations where people can live.

Essential features include: a power source, engine, thrusters to change direction, a computer and antennae for sending and receiving messages from Earth.

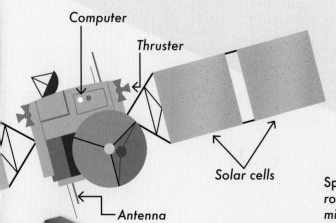

Computer

Thruster

Solar cells

Antenna

TIMELINE OF SPACECRAFT

1957

Russia launches the first satellite – Sputnik – into space (see pages 6–7).

1969

Saturn 5 rocket blasts Neil Armstrong and Buzz Aldrin into space on a mission that makes them the first humans to walk on the Moon (see pages 10–11).

1977

Voyager 1 and Voyager 2 are launched into space. They are now the furthest travelled spacecraft (see pages 14–15).

1990

Building work on the International Space Station (ISS) starts.

1998

In 2000, the first astronauts from USA and Russia begin living on board (see pages 22–23).

2001

The extraordinary Wilkinson Microwave Anisotropy Probe (WMAP) spacecraft is launched to scan space and unlock the secrets of how and when the Universe began (see pages 24–25).

2003

Spirit and Opportunity, the planetary rover vehicles, arrive on Mars on their mission to explore the planet closest to Earth (see pages 26–27).

1958
1961
1962
1971
1981
2004
2035

SPACE AGENCIES

A space agency is a government-funded program bringing together some of the best and brightest minds to plan and accomplish space missions. Today, over 70 countries have space agencies, the most famous being NASA. Space agencies often work together, sharing expertise and information. The Cassini-Huygens mission to Saturn, launched in 1997, involved 260 scientists from 17 countries, as well as thousands of other experts that took part in the design, engineering, flying and data collection.

IN ORBIT

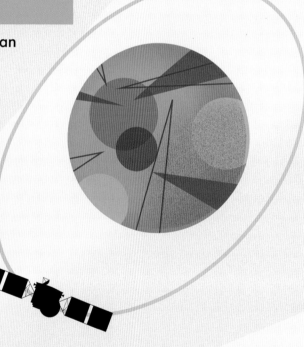

An orbit is the path that an object follows around another object in space, repeated over and over again. Objects in space that orbit around other objects are called satellites. They can be natural or artificial. They stay in orbit because of the effect of gravity. Gravity is an invisible force between objects, that pulls objects towards each other.

Gravity keeps a satellite in orbit by pulling the satellite towards Earth, but because the satellite is moving sideways very fast, it does not fall to Earth and instead falls into a circular path (orbit) around Earth. In effect, satellites are constantly falling around and around Earth, until they slow down, when gravity pulls them to Earth.

SPUTNIK 1

The first spacecraft to orbit Earth was a tiny silver satellite called Sputnik 1. It orbited Earth for three months in 1957, emitting a 'beep, beep' signal.

BUILDING BRIEF

Design and build a satellite that can orbit the Earth. What it does is not so important – being the first one up in space is what it's all about!

Engineer: Sergei Korolev

Chief constructor: Mikhail S Khomyakov

Sputnik 1 was spherical, like a planet. It measured 58 cm in diameter.

BEEP, BEEP

The power for the tiny craft and radio transmitter came from three silver-zinc batteries.

The outer shell was made from polished aluminium, so that it could reflect sunlight and be seen from Earth.

It had four antennae that stuck out from the body of the satellite.

SPACE RACE

In August 1957 the USA announced that it was close to launching the first satellite into space. Russia, then part of the USSR, wanted to be the first country to explore space and had been planning to launch a big and heavy satellite. However, in order to beat the USA they decided to quickly assemble something much smaller and Sputnik 1 was launched on 4 October, four months before the USA's first satellite, Explorer 1.

THE LAUNCH CRAFT

To get Sputnik 1 into orbit, an enormous rocket, called R-7, was needed. Rocket engines burn large amounts of fuel and oxygen – the resulting high-pressure exhaust gas is released at the bottom, pushing the rocket off the ground and thrusting it into the air. It's like letting the air out of a balloon.

A rocket needs to travel at over 40,000 km/h to break away from the Earth's gravitational pull.

Nose cone
Once R-7 had reached about 220 km above Earth, the nose cone popped open and Sputnik 1 sprung out on the next part of its journey.

← Core rocket

Engines
The R-7 featured a core rocket with its own engine and four extra booster engines around the sides.

R 7

← Booster engines

Height 30 m

SPUTNIK 1'S JOURNEY

Sputnik 1 travelled around Earth for 92 days, until its batteries ran out. Discoveries made and tested during the orbit were limited, but important.

• It proved that spacecraft could be sent outside Earth's atmosphere and maintain an orbit.
• Scientists learnt how radio waves travelled back to Earth.
• Scientists could measure the density of the atmosphere as the satellite travelled through it.

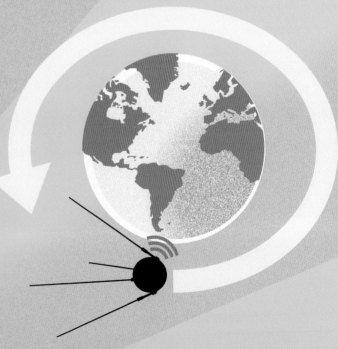

Sputnik 1 travelled at 29,000 km/h and went around Earth 1,440 times. Each complete orbit took 98 minutes. When the batteries failed, it lost momentum, causing it to be pulled back down by Earth's gravity, burning up in the atmosphere as it fell.

VOSTOK 1

The first human launched into space was Yuri Gagarin. He left Earth on 21 April 1961 on Vostok 1, a launch rocket that contained his capsule, Vostok 3KA. Once in space, the released capsule took 106 minutes to complete one historic orbit of Earth, 169 km above the ground, before coming back down.

STAGE 1

BUILDING BRIEF

Launch a rocket capable of carrying a human into space, orbiting Earth and carrying them safely back home again. Be the first country in the world to achieve this.

Space agency:
Soviet Space Program

Stage 1:
Four booster rockets burnt their fuel up after two minutes, then fell away.

Stage 2 (top right):
The core engine blazed for 30 seconds before being ejected.

Stage 3 (right):
The remaining part of the craft sped on at 8 km per minute. Ten minutes into the flight, it ejected the Vostok 3KA capsule into orbit.

VOSTOK 1

THE ROCKET

The Vostok 1 rocket was similar in design to the Sputnik rocket, the R-7. It worked in three spectacular stages to thrust Yuri Gagarin and the Vostok 3KA space capsule into space.

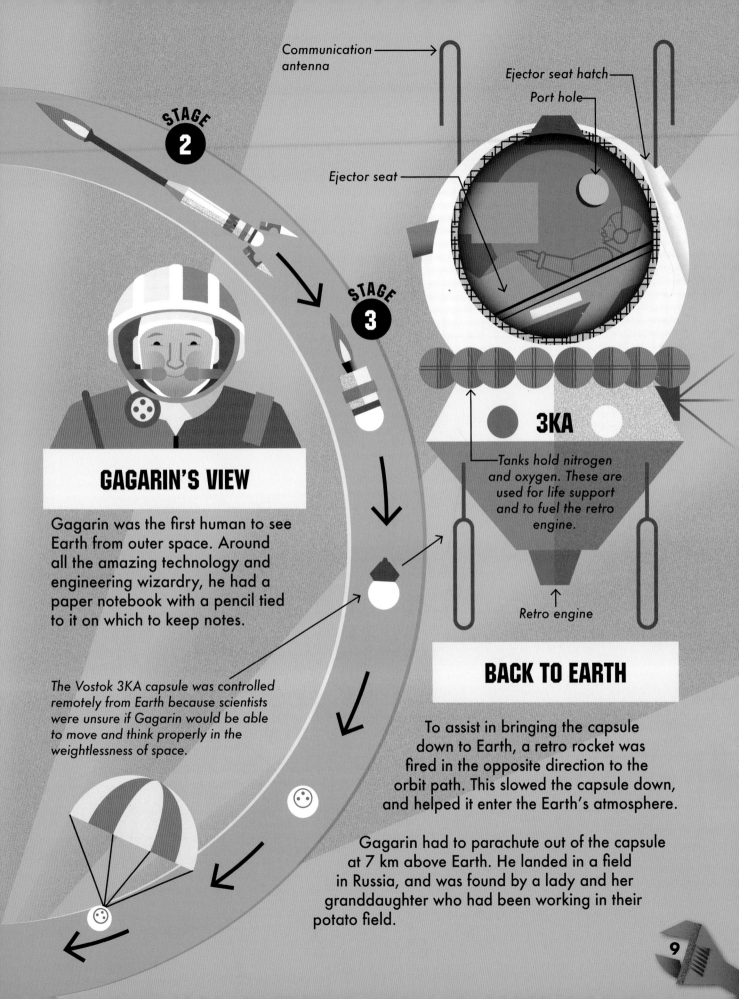

Communication antenna

Ejector seat hatch

Port hole

Ejector seat

STAGE 2

STAGE 3

GAGARIN'S VIEW

Gagarin was the first human to see Earth from outer space. Around all the amazing technology and engineering wizardry, he had a paper notebook with a pencil tied to it on which to keep notes.

The Vostok 3KA capsule was controlled remotely from Earth because scientists were unsure if Gagarin would be able to move and think properly in the weightlessness of space.

3KA

Tanks hold nitrogen and oxygen. These are used for life support and to fuel the retro engine.

Retro engine

BACK TO EARTH

To assist in bringing the capsule down to Earth, a retro rocket was fired in the opposite direction to the orbit path. This slowed the capsule down, and helped it enter the Earth's atmosphere.

Gagarin had to parachute out of the capsule at 7 km above Earth. He landed in a field in Russia, and was found by a lady and her granddaughter who had been working in their potato field.

SATURN 5

The Apollo 11 mission to take the first humans to the Moon, launched in 1969. It used the Saturn 5 rocket, the command module *Columbia* and the lunar module *Eagle* to get the astronauts into space, onto the Moon, and back down to Earth safely.

BUILDING BRIEF

Design and build the spacecraft and equipment needed to get humans to the Moon, and back down again to Earth safely.

Space agency: NASA

Saturn 5 chief engineer: Wernher von Braun

SATURN 5 ROCKET

The success of the Apollo 11 mission relied on the rocket power of Saturn 5 – it was the tallest and heaviest rocket ever built. Saturn 5 worked in three stages.

Stage 1 had five F1 engines, featuring a single combustion chamber burning liquid fuel. This is the most powerful rocket engine ever built. When the fuel burnt up it dropped away and stage 2 began.

Stage 2 featured five J2 rocket engines. The engines burnt liquid hydrogen and liquid oxygen. These fuels worked well in the high atmosphere where it is colder, keeping the fuels in their liquid state, but not cold enough to freeze them.

Stage 3 had one J2 engine, which fired once, to put Apollo 11 into a low Earth orbit then stopped. Once the Earth, Moon and spacecraft were in the correct positions, it fired again, taking *Columbia* and *Eagle* to the Moon.

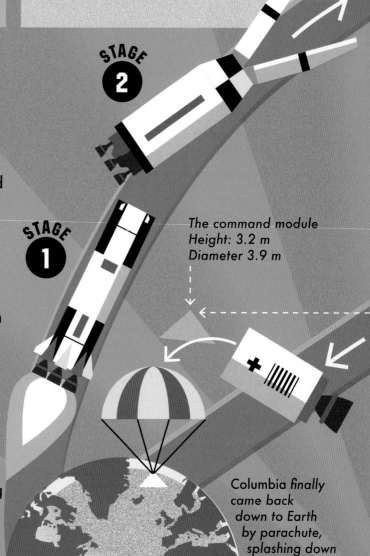

STAGE 2

STAGE 1

The command module
Height: 3.2 m
Diameter 3.9 m

Columbia finally came back down to Earth by parachute, splashing down in the sea.

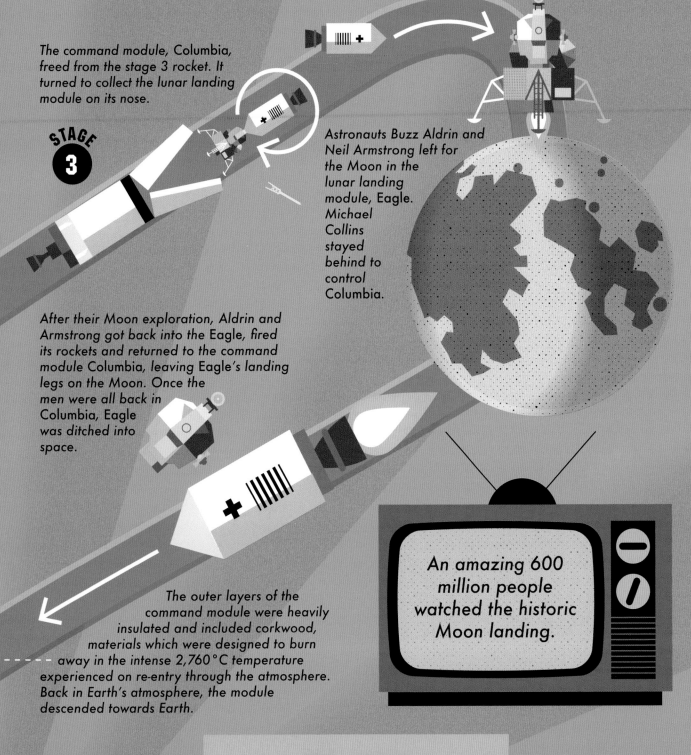

The command module, Columbia, freed from the stage 3 rocket. It turned to collect the lunar landing module on its nose.

STAGE 3

Astronauts Buzz Aldrin and Neil Armstrong left for the Moon in the lunar landing module, Eagle. Michael Collins stayed behind to control Columbia.

After their Moon exploration, Aldrin and Armstrong got back into the Eagle, fired its rockets and returned to the command module Columbia, leaving Eagle's landing legs on the Moon. Once the men were all back in Columbia, Eagle was ditched into space.

The outer layers of the command module were heavily insulated and included corkwood, materials which were designed to burn away in the intense 2,760°C temperature experienced on re-entry through the atmosphere. Back in Earth's atmosphere, the module descended towards Earth.

An amazing 600 million people watched the historic Moon landing.

FUEL CELLS

Electric power for the spacecraft was provided by hydrogen and oxygen fuel cells. When hydrogen and oxygen mix in the cell, energy is released that can be converted to electric power. The clever part of this process is that mixing hydrogen and oxygen creates water, and this water was drunk by the astronauts on the trip!

LUNAR ROVING VEHICLE

Nicknamed moon buggies, lunar roving vehicles (LRVs) were built for three of the Apollo space missions in 1971 and 1972. Easily transportable LRVs meant that when astronauts landed on the Moon they could drive around and explore a greater area.

BUILDING BRIEF

Design and build a vehicle to be driven on the Moon. It must be strong enough to cope with the lunar landscape.

Space agency: NASA

Location of abandoned vehicles: There are three Apollo moon buggies that have been left behind on the Moon.

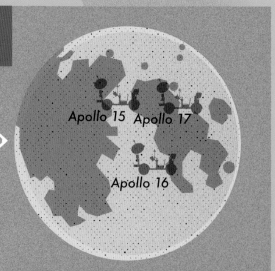

Apollo 15 Apollo 17

Apollo 16

STOWAWAY

The way of carrying the buggy to the Moon was inspired – it was hidden away in the wall of the lunar module craft and popped out on landing, ready to rove!

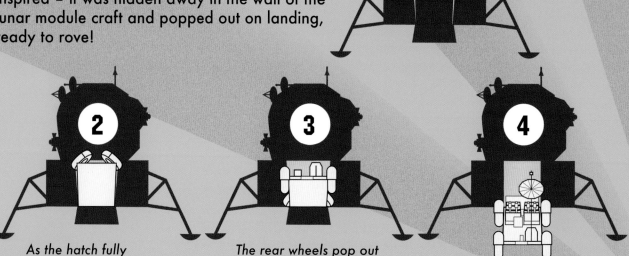

1 Astronauts pull hatch open.

2 As the hatch fully opens, the front wheels pop out first.

3 The rear wheels pop out as the hatch is lowered.

4 The astronauts pull the rover clear of the lunar module.

LONGEST MOON BUGGY JOURNEYS

The LRV could only travel a short distance from the landing craft in case it broke down and the astronaut had to walk back.

LRV:	Longest single journey:
Apollo 15	12.47 km
Apollo 16	11.59 km
Apollo 17	20.12 km

Astronaut Eugene A Cernan driving a lunar rover on the Apollo 17 mission.

Included seat belts fastened with Velcro.

Contained a tool bag with a hammer, scoop, brush and rake for collecting rock samples.

The tyres were covered in zinc wire mesh for improved grip.

The buggy could carry two people on fold-down seats.

Each of the four wheels had a battery-driven motor.

RUGGED ROVER

Lunar rover vehicles had to be super tough to cope with the bumpy, dusty surface, and lightweight enough for the command module to carry them. The main frame was made from aluminium alloy tubing and weighed just 204 kg. The exterior had to be able to withstand the extreme temperatures experienced in space, from –100° C to +120° C.

VoYAGErs 1 ANd 2

The Voyager 1 and Voyager 2 spacecraft launched within a few days of each other aboard separate Titan-Centaur rockets. They set off in 1977 with a mission to fly further into space than any other spacecraft, right to the edge of the Sun's reach and possibly beyond. They have now been exploring space for over 40 years and are still going strong.

BUILDING BRIEF

Build a craft that can journey far into space. It will need to collect information on the major planets, then travel on for as long as it can, exploring the far reaches of the solar system and beyond.

Project scientist: Ed Stone

Space agency: NASA

It takes 13 hours for signals from the Voyagers to get back to Earth.

VOYAGER TWINS

Voyagers 1 and 2 are identical. Their antennae are always pointing towards Earth so they can radio back their findings. They measure and collect various kinds of data, such as:
• the speed of solar winds
• magnetic fields with their magnetometer
• cosmic rays with their cosmic ray sub system.

They each have a tiny amount of memory storage; the average mobile phone has 240,000 times more storage power. The signals they send also have a tiny amount of power – the same as a refrigerator bulb!

In 2017, Voyager 1 was 20.6 billion km from the Sun, while Voyager 2 was 17 billion km away.

MAIN MISSIONS

Each Voyager was tasked to fly past different planets and moons in our solar system.

Voyager 1's achievements:
- *It flew past Jupiter and its moons, discovering volcanoes on the surface of the moon Io.*
- *It flew past Saturn and its moons; it sent back images of icy surfaces on the moons, proving there is water elsewhere in the galaxy.*
- *It also took the first image of the Earth and our Moon together.*

Voyager 2's achievements:
- *It flew past Jupiter and Saturn and their moons.*
- *It sent back the first close up images of Uranus and Neptune.*
- *It discovered there were rings around Uranus and 10 new moons.*
- *It found Neptune has four rings and found five new moons.*

Their next goal is to continue deeper into space on the Voyager Interstellar Mission (VIM). They will travel outside the area of magnetic force from the Sun, known as the heliosphere, going through the heliosheath boundary and on to interstellar space.

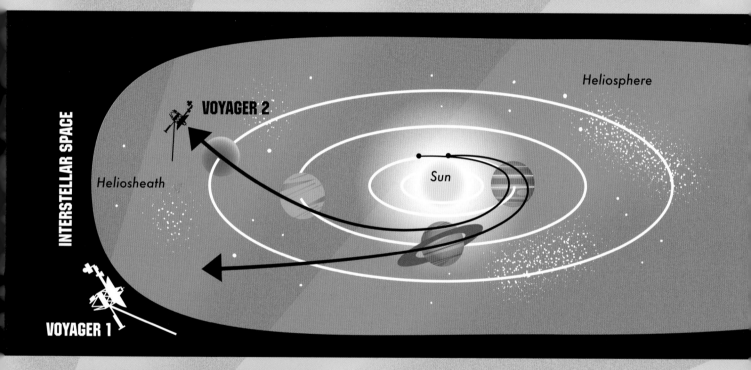

POWER SOURCE

The Voyagers have amazingly little power, although their journey has been the longest for any craft in history. Power is supplied by three radioisotope thermoelectric generators. These use thermocouples – two pieces of different metal wire that are heated by the radioactive metal plutonium. They warm at different temperatures, producing a volt between the wires that is converted to electric power. It's a source of power that needs no moveable parts. They will generate power until 2020, after which the Voyagers will drift in space, but on the same course.

THERMOCOUPLE

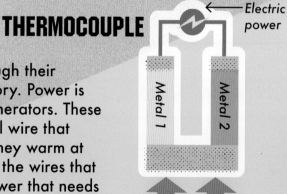

Heat released by the radioactive decay of plutonium

SPACE SHUTTLE

The first space shuttle, launched in 1981, was a feat of technical ingenuity. It was a spacecraft that was not only reusable, but could take off like a rocket and land like an aircraft! The space shuttle was also the first winged spacecraft to orbit Earth.

BUILDING BRIEF

Build a reusable spacecraft to enable the launch of future space missions and the construction of a space station.

Space agency: NASA

LIFT OFF

The orange external tank (ET) fed fuel to the shuttle's main engines, while the solid rocket boosters (SRBs) strapped to the side provided additional thrust. The SRBs fired until the shuttle reached an altitude of 45 km above the ground; they then detached and fell to Earth using parachutes, and were recovered for future use. The now nearly empty tank separated and fell in a preplanned trajectory (path) with the majority of it disintegrating in the atmosphere and the rest falling into the ocean.

It took 8.5 minutes for the space shuttle, called an Orbiter, to reach space, and once there, it powered itself with its own fuel and engines.

The huge fuel tank used to be painted white, but this added extra weight, so they decided to leave it in its original colour – bright orange!

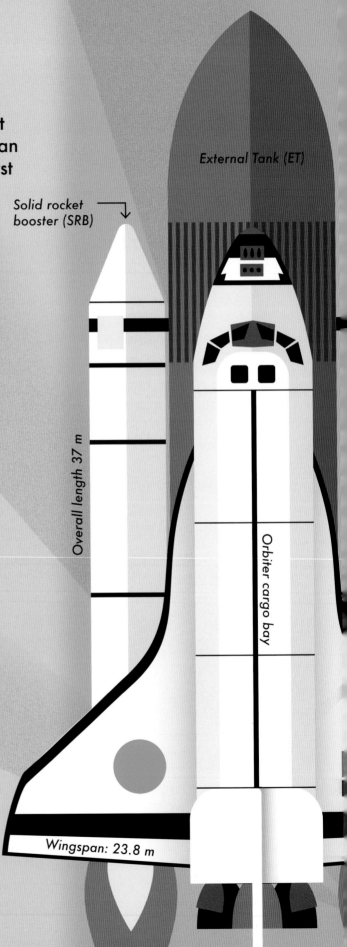

External Tank (ET)

Solid rocket booster (SRB)

Overall length 37 m

Orbiter cargo bay

Wingspan: 23.8 m

CANADARM

Canadarm was the shuttle's robotic arm system; it was 15 m long and had six joints to mimic the movement of a human arm. Extending out from the orbiter cargo bay and controlled by computer, it was used for lifting, climbing, grabbing satellites out of the sky, and even tapping ice off the outside of the orbiter on frosty days!

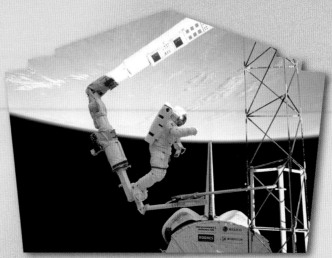

Canadarm in action

LOOPY LANDING

The Orbiter had to start preparing to land halfway round Earth from where it landed. This is because it needed the distance to slow down its momentum. During descent it flipped over to fly upside down, firing retro rockets backwards to slow it down. It flipped in the air and descended at 40 degrees through the atmosphere. Finally, on the runway, a parachute opened to help slow the craft down.

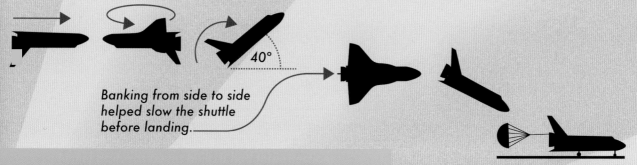

40°

Banking from side to side helped slow the shuttle before landing.

MOVEABLE ENGINE NOZZLES

The space shuttle had three exhaust nozzles where the gases from the burning fuel escaped. This gas pushed the rocket forward. The nozzles are moveable which allowed the orbiter to use the force of the gas to help steer and control the direction in which it travelled. They moved on a gimbal, a device that has a fixed axis with circles that rotate around, allowing for controlled movement of the engines when the rocket is moving and vibrating.

Fixed axis

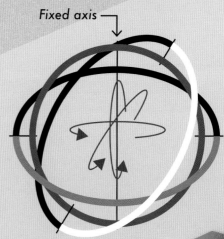

Gimbal

17

HUBBLE SPACE TELESCOPE

The Hubble Space Telescope was launched from the space shuttle *Discovery* in 1990. It orbits at 537 km above the Earth's atmosphere and travels at an incredible 27,350 km/h. Hubble has sent back amazing images that have changed the way we think about space.

BUILDING BRIEF

Design a telescope that can work in space, with a super-strong lens that can record images free from the distractions of light and weather.

Space agency: NASA

CASSEGRAIN REFLECTOR

Hubble is a cassegrain reflector telescope – it has two mirrors inside, one convex, one concave. These reflect and intensify the outside view then direct it to an on-board computer. The glass of the main concave mirror had to be polished for two years before the aluminium backing was added to turn it into a mirror.

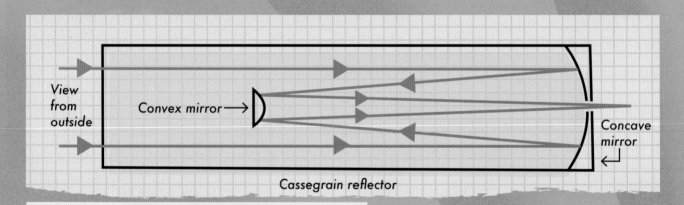

View from outside | Convex mirror → | Concave mirror ↵

Cassegrain reflector

DATA TRANSFER

Hubble's data makes a complicated journey back to Earth. It goes from the Hubble computer via its transmitter to a space satellite. A giant receiver dish on the ground in New Mexico, USA, moves to track the satellite and picks up the signal. From here, the data goes to the Goddard Space Flight Center near Washington D.C., USA and finally to the Hubble headquarters at the Space Telescope Science Institute in Baltimore, USA, where the information is stored and analysed.

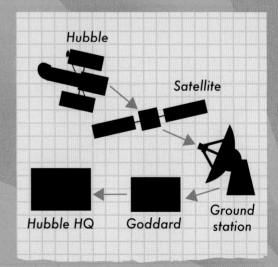

Hubble
Satellite
Hubble HQ | Goddard | Ground station

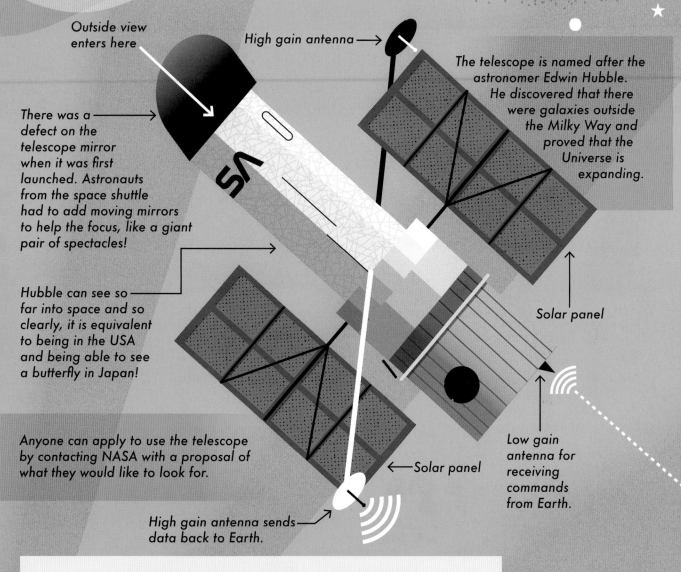

Outside view enters here

High gain antenna →

The telescope is named after the astronomer Edwin Hubble. He discovered that there were galaxies outside the Milky Way and proved that the Universe is expanding.

There was a defect on the telescope mirror when it was first launched. Astronauts from the space shuttle had to add moving mirrors to help the focus, like a giant pair of spectacles!

Hubble can see so far into space and so clearly, it is equivalent to being in the USA and being able to see a butterfly in Japan!

Solar panel

Anyone can apply to use the telescope by contacting NASA with a proposal of what they would like to look for.

Low gain antenna for receiving commands from Earth.

← Solar panel

High gain antenna sends data back to Earth.

SPECTACULAR HUBBLE SNAPSHOTS

A shot of Neptune showing light and dark vortex clouds.

The death of a star forming a rotten egg shape in the Calabash Nebula.

Pillars of gas and dust as stars are created in the Carina Nebula.

19

ROSETTA SPACE PROBE

The Rosetta space probe was launched in 2004 as part of a 10-year mission to follow and study a comet called 67P/Churyumov-Gerasimenko. The probe was looking for signs of life on comets and planets.

BUILDING BRIEF

Design and build a spacecraft that can chase and study a comet across thousands of kilometres, carrying a small lander that will ultimately end up on the moving comet.

Space agency: European Space Agency

Solar panels

ORBIT ADVENTURE

The Rosetta probe is a small aluminium box with solar cell-covered wings that provided its power. This tiny craft travelled for 10 years in a complex series of orbits that helped it to gain speed and the right position to catch its comet. It had to go round the Sun three times, gathering momentum from the gravity on Earth and Mars to then gain a larger orbit.

The Rosetta spacecraft had to reach speeds of 55,000 km/h to travel alongside the 67P comet, taking amazing photos of the surface.

Rosetta

Comet

Sun

Mars

Earth

1 2 3

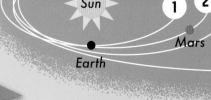

EXPERIMENTS

The Rosetta probe, along with its landing module, Philae, ran 11 different experiments, analysing temperature, atmosphere and gravity, as well as collecting dust and gases. Rosetta found oxygen and nitrogen and the amino acid glycine – an organic compound that could have brought life to planets.

The experiment instruments were set on top of Rosetta, so they could catch information from the speeding comet.

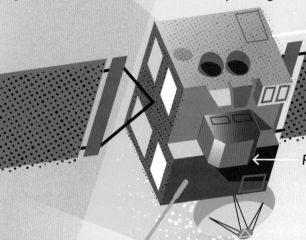

← *Philae lander*

PHILAE LANDER

The small robotic Philae lander was released from Rosetta and landed on the comet on 12 November 2014 – it was an enormous technical achievement. It didn't land in a perfect position but did manage to send back images and data about the surface rock.

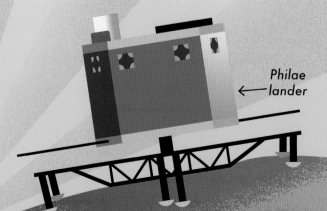

← *Philae lander*

In 2016, Rosetta purposely crashed into the comet as its power was failing.

INTERNATIONAL SPACE STATION

The International Space Station (ISS) is the only permanently inhabited craft in space and is an amazing example of what can be achieved by combining the technical talents and expertise of many nations.

BUILDING BRIEF

Design and build a space station in which people can live and work together for long periods of time in zero gravity.

Space agency: NASA and 15 other national agencies

GIANT SPACE JIGSAW

The ISS is a giant floating science laboratory in space. It was put together in space; construction started in 1998, when the first piece was put into orbit during a Russian mission. It took over 115 space flights to deliver the rest of the components and build the ISS. In total, there are 38 modules that fit together like a giant jigsaw. These contain laboratories, a fitness area, and everything else the crew will need, including a bathroom!

LEARNING LAB

So much has been studied and learnt aboard the ISS; experiments have included:

 growing plants

 studying fire

 studying the effects of living in zero gravity

 observing dark matter and cosmic rays

 observing changes in the Earth's atmosphere.

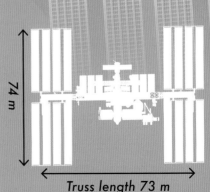

74 m

Truss length 73 m

SUCCESSFUL SPACE SHAPES

The ISS is made up of many different shaped components, all designed to be the best shape and structure for their job.

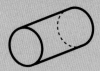

The modules where the astronauts live and work are cylinders or spheres, shapes that are good for a pressurised interior, like a fizzy drinks can.

The panels holding the solar cells are flat and wide, to collect as much power from the Sun as possible.

The central modules and solar panels are connected by a strong backbone made from a network of triangular latticed titanium, called a truss. Lattice structures are used on bridges because of their structural strength.

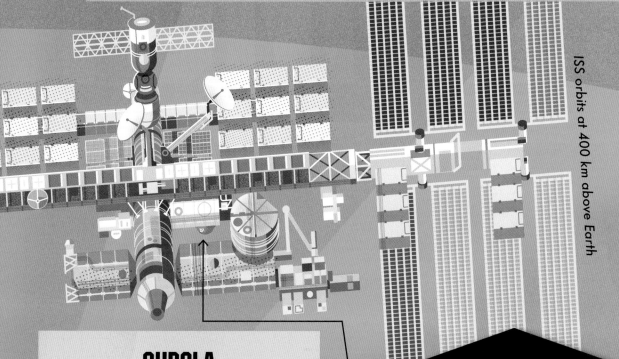

ISS orbits at 400 km above Earth

CUPOLA

One of the modules, the cupola node, is used for observation and sits on the Earth-facing side of the station. The cupola gives an all-round view of incoming crafts and outside operations. It's the control centre for the manipulator arm, which is used for the loading and unloading of cargo, catching and repairing satellites and as an anchor for astronauts working outside.

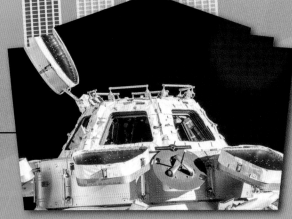

The cupola's windowpanes are made from specially strengthened glass and have shutters to protect them from flying space debris.

WILKINSON MICROWAVE ANISOTROPY PROBE

The Wilkinson Microwave Anisotropy Probe (WMAP) was an awesome small craft that, until 2010, scanned the sky looking for clues to answer big questions, such as how old is the Universe? What is it made from? How has it changed? And the answers are amazing!

BUILDING BRIEF

Design and build a spacecraft to reach an orbit that can look into deep space to find cosmic radiation left over from the Big Bang.

Space agency: NASA with John Hopkins and Princeton University

CENTRIPETAL ORBIT

WMAP was launched in 2001 with a complex looping journey to help it gain enough speed to swing out towards a distant region of space called Lagrange 2. At this point in space, its orbit was not around a planet, but like the end of a swinging pendulum instead. This is called a centripetal orbit. WMAP used the gravitational force of the Earth, Moon and Sun to achieve this orbit.

WMAP faced away from the Sun and scanned outwards, looking for heat remaining from the beginning of the Universe. As it orbited, the front moved around so it could scan 360 degrees at a time.

Lunar orbit

WMAP orbit

Spin direction

Sight

Gregorian optics and separate reflectors

Sight

Centripetal orbit

Size 3.6 m x 5.1 m

1.5 million km

Solar panels faced towards the Sun, while WMAP's umbrella shape shaded the equipment from the Sun's rays.

SKY SCANNER

WMAP used two back-to-back Gregorian telescopes that scan for cosmic microwave background radiation, recorded as temperature. Taking two sets of information at a time meant they could be compared, like measuring two pieces of string next to each other. Readings were channelled into the telescopes by reflectors, and then bounced back and forth on the mirrors inside to intensify the readings.

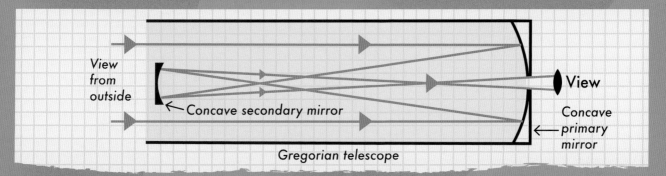

View from outside

← Concave secondary mirror

View

Concave primary mirror

Gregorian telescope

DYNAMIC DISCOVERIES

This tiny machine made amazing discoveries. WMAP was able to date the Universe to when it began: 13.77 billion years ago! It drew a map of the Universe from its beginning to now. This showed that the Universe is expanding and that the expansion is speeding up.

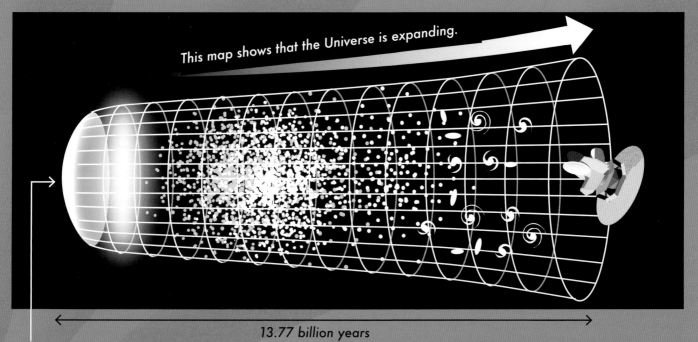

This map shows that the Universe is expanding.

13.77 billion years

The map shows the point at which stars started to shine, when the Universe was 200 million years old!

It also shows what the Universe is made of: 4.6 per cent atoms, 24 per cent dark matter and 71.4 per cent dark energy.

SPIRIT AND OPPORTUNITY MARS ROVERS

Robotic explorers named *Spirit* and *Opportunity* were sent to Mars in 2003. The rovers' mission was to study Martian geology. To do this they rolled for kilometre after kilometre across the surface of the planet, examining rocks and minerals on the way.

BUILDING BRIEF

Design and build planet explorers to search the surface of Mars, collecting rocks and hunting for evidence of water.

Space agency: NASA

Cameras record finds and send them back to Earth via radio transmitter.

The solar panels can only charge for four hours in the Martian sunlight, but this provides enough power for each day's roving.

Tool arm

There are three wheels on each side, attached to a rocker-bogie.

ROCKER-BOGIE

The surface of Mars is very rocky, so each rover uses a special mechanism called a rocker-bogie that helps them to tackle rough terrain without shaking the rover's body about too much.

Pivoting arms connected to the six wheels allow them all to stay on the ground. The rocking motion of the wheels actually helps to keep the instruments on top level as it travels.

1.5 m high
2.3 m wide
1.6 m long
Weighs 180 kg

The rovers have six wheels; each wheel has a deep tread, like a cog wheel, rather than a tyre.

Each wheel is connected to a motor and can move forward and back and turn to move in any direction, giving the best traction over the rocky terrain.

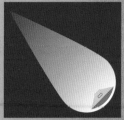

Capsule enters Mars' atmosphere

Parachute and rockets slow capsule

Airbags deploy

Pod lands and bounces

Airbags deflate and pod opens

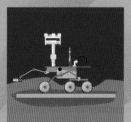

Ready to go!

CRASH LANDING

The rovers were launched into space in June and July of 2003. It took under seven months for them to reach their orbit around Mars. The mission needed to follow a careful process to deliver them safely to the Martian surface.

First, a stiff heat shield called an aeroshell and a parachute were used to slow the lander down as it plummeted towards Mars. Retro rockets were fired to make it go even slower. Airbags were inflated to cushion the lander as it landed. Once it had bounced to a halt, the airbags deflated. Finally, the lander's petals were designed to open up in such a way that the rover would always be the right way up, no matter which way it landed. Once the rover had charged its solar-power batteries, it was ready to start its Martian mission!

FINDINGS

The rovers sent pictures back to Earth via a radio transmitter. Among their important discoveries were magnetic dust, meteorites, and evidence of water. *Spirit* ended communications in 2010, but *Opportunity* carries on rolling!

This image above was taken by Opportunity in March 2015. It shows the surface of Mars and a large crater which scientists named Spirit of St Louis Crater in honour of Charles Lindbergh, who in 1927 became the first person to fly non-stop across the Atlantic in his aeroplane – Spirit of St Louis.

FASCINATING FACTS

Spacecraft and space exploration have inspired many engineering inventions. But did you know how many have been adapted for use on Earth?

*Many **smartphone cameras** use digital technology that was invented by NASA for use on space missions.*

Joysticks *can be used to play video games, but they were first used to steer moon buggies.*

Cordless drills *were developed by NASA for collecting Moon samples on Apollo missions.*

TRAVEL DISTANCES OF CRAFT

New Horizons space probe was launched in 2007 with the primary objective of flying to Pluto to send back information on this as-yet-unexplored dwarf planet. It sent back amazing photos and is now heading towards its next destination in the Kuiper Belt.

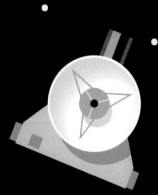

7   8   9   10   11   12   13

Billion km from the Sun

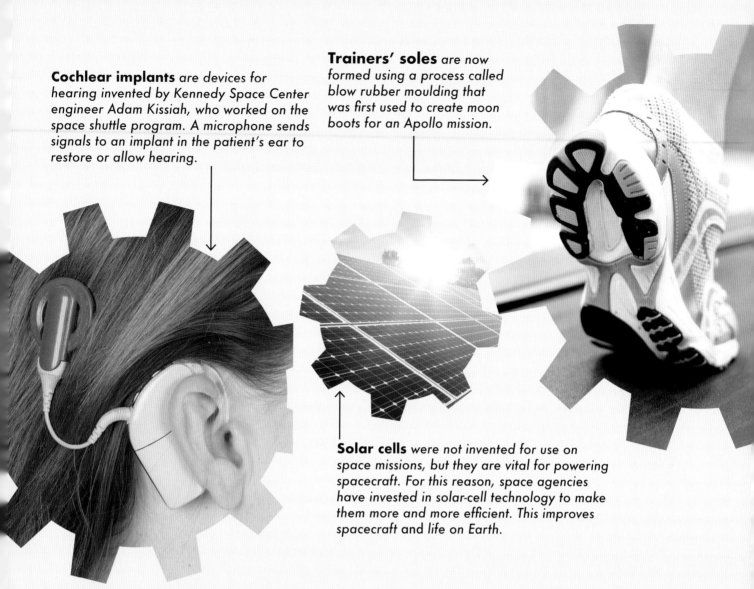

Cochlear implants are devices for hearing invented by Kennedy Space Center engineer Adam Kissiah, who worked on the space shuttle program. A microphone sends signals to an implant in the patient's ear to restore or allow hearing.

Trainers' soles are now formed using a process called blow rubber moulding that was first used to create moon boots for an Apollo mission.

Solar cells were not invented for use on space missions, but they are vital for powering spacecraft. For this reason, space agencies have invested in solar-cell technology to make them more and more efficient. This improves spacecraft and life on Earth.

Pioneer 11, launched in 1973, flew past Saturn and sent back pictures revealing two new moons and another ring.

Pioneer 10, launched in 1972, flew to Jupiter and then beyond. It was the first spacecraft to fly through the asteroid belt and it sent signals back for 30 years.

Voyager 2

Voyager 1

15   16   17   18   19   20   21

Billion km from the Sun

FURTHER INFORMATION

BOOKS

How to Design the World's Best Space Station in 10 Simple Steps by Paul Mason (Wayland, 2016)

Planet Earth: Journey into Space by Michael Bright (Wayland, 2016)

Professor Astro Cat's Frontiers of Space by Dr. Dominic Walliman and Ben Newman (Flying Eye Books, 2013)

The Usborne Big Book of Rockets and Spacecraft by Louie Stowell (Usborne, 2015)

What's Inside: Spacecraft by David West (Franklin Watts, 2016)

WEBSITES

This site has information about space, especially written for children:
http://www.spacekids.co.uk/learn/

The NASA and ESA sites have information and amazing pictures about their missions:
https://www.nasa.gov/
http://www.esa.int/ESA

The BBC Newsround website has information and films about spacecraft:
http://www.bbc.co.uk/cbbc/search?q=spacecraft

The International Space Station (ISS) is the third brightest thing visible in the night sky after the Sun and Moon. You can find out when it is passing your way via this link:
http://www.spaceflight.nasa.gov/realdata/sightings/index.html

A cool website that tracks what astronauts on the ISS can see:
http://iss.astroviewer.net

Every effort has been made by the Publishers to ensure that these websites are suitable for children, that they are of the highest educational value, and that they contain no inappropriate or offensive material. However, because of the nature of the Internet, it is impossible to guarantee that the contents of these sites will not be altered. We strongly advise that Internet access is supervised by a responsible adult.

GLOSSARY

aluminium *A lightweight, silvery metal that does not rust.*

amino acids *The substances which combine to form proteins.*

antenna (plural antennae) *A metal rod that can send or receive radio wave messages.*

asteroid belt *Part of the solar system where rocky asteroids are in orbit.*

atmosphere *The layers of gases that surround a planet such as Earth.*

atom *A tiny particle of matter – the building block from which everything is made.*

combustion *The process of burning, when fuel mixes with oxygen to produce light and heat.*

comet *An object made from rock, dust and ice that moves around the Sun and looks like a star with a tail.*

communication *Passing information between people or machines.*

cupola *A rounded dome.*

dark energy/dark matter *The invisible energy and matter that scientists can't detect but which they believe is out in space.*

defect *A problem or fault.*

descent *Downward movement.*

ejector seat *A seat that can propel the sitter to safety out of a spacecraft or aeroplane, using a small explosion.*

engineer *Someone who designs, constructs and maintains buildings, machines and other structures.*

exhaust *Waste gases or fumes that come from a working engine.*

galaxy *A collection of millions of stars, gas and dust held together by gravitational forces. Our solar system is part of the galaxy called the Milky Way.*

gravitational force *The strong pulling force of gravity.*

gravity *The invisible force of attraction between all objects. Earth's gravity keeps our feet on the ground and makes objects fall to the ground.*

ingenuity *Being clever, inventive and original.*

inhabited *Of a place or landscape, occupied or lived in by people or animals.*

interstellar space *In our solar system, the place in space beyond the magnetic field of the Sun.*

Kuiper Belt *An area of the outer solar system, beyond Neptune, filled with asteroids, comets and dwarf planets.*

laboratory *A room or building designed for scientific experiments, research and lessons.*

lunar *To do with the Moon.*

momentum *The tendency of a moving object to keep moving in the same direction.*

nebula *A cloud of gases and dust out of which a star is created.*

orbit *The path followed by a planet, satellite or other body in space.*

radiation *Energy travelling as electromagnetic waves.*

radio waves *A type of electromagnetic wave. It is very useful for long-distance communication.*

reflector *An object that reflects light or sound waves.*

solar cell *A device that turns sunlight into energy.*

solar panel *A panel designed to absorb sunlight and change it into electrical energy.*

solar system *The planets, comets and asteroids, including Earth, that orbit the Sun.*

space mission *A journey or expedition into space to gather information.*

stages (of a rocket) *Separate sections of a rocket, each with their own rocket engines.*

technology *Machinery or ideas developed from the latest scientific discoveries.*

telescope *A device that uses mirrors to magnify objects over long distances to make them visible to the human eye.*

thrust *The force generated in engines which overcomes the weight of a rocket or plane to move it through the air.*

titanium *A strong but light grey metal that does not rust easily.*

traction *The force that causes a moving object to stick against the surface it is moving along.*

trajectory *The curved path followed by an object through the air or through space.*

Universe *The vast expanse of space, and everything that exists in it.*

vibrating *The fast, shaking, to and fro movements of an object.*

INDEX

Awesome ENGINEERING

TITLES IN THIS SERIES:

BRIDGES

Get Over It!
Si-o-she Pol
Brooklyn Bridge
Forth Bridge
Vizcaya Bridge
Tower Bridge
Golden Gate Bridge
Governor Albert D Rosellini Bridge
Akashi-Kaikyō Bridge
Juscelino Kubitschek Bridge
Millau Viaduct
The Helix
Fascinating Facts
Further Information
Glossary
Index

FAIRGROUND RIDES

All the Fun of the Fair!
Swingboats
Mauch Chunk Switchback Railway
Carousel
Chair Swing Ride
Ferris Wheel
Bumper Cars
Big Dipper
Orbiter
Slingshot
Kingda Ka and Zumanjaro
Eejanaika
Fascinating Facts
Further Information
Glossary
Index

SKYSCRAPERS

Build It Tall
Home Insurance Building
Chrysler Building
Empire State Building
Willis Tower
Petronas Twin Tower
30 St Mary Axe
Taipei 101
Bahrain World Trade Center
Burj Khalifa
Bosco Verticale
Shanghai Tower
Fascinating Facts
Further Information
Glossary
Index

SPACECRAFT

Out of This World!
Sputnik 1
Vostock 1
Apollo 11
Lunar Roving Vehicle
Voyager 1 and 2
Space Shuttle
Hubble Telescope
Rosetta Mission
International Space Station
Wilkinson Microwave Anisotropy Probe
Spirit and Opportunity Mars Rover
Fascinating Facts
Further Information
Glossary
Index

TRAINS, PLANES AND SHIPS

On the Move
Mary Rose
Washington Paddle Steamer
Stephenson's Rocket
SS Great Britain
Wright Flyer
Heinkel He 178
Shinkansen Bullet Train
Concorde
Shanghai Maglev Train
Airbus A380
USS Gerald R Ford (CVN 78)
Fascinating Facts
Further Information
Glossary
Index

TUNNELS

Going Underground
Thames Tunnel
New York City Subway
Holland Tunnel
Seikan Tunnel
Channel Tunnel
Oresund Tunnel
Laerdal Tunnel
Boston Big Dig Project
Smart Tunnel
Hadron Collider Tunnel
Gotthard Base Tunnel
Fascinating Facts
Further Information
Glossary
Index